I0492480

THOUGHTS OF FASHION AND MORE

If all else fails, at least we will always have our designer labels and fashion skills.
Page 4

If all else fails, at least we will always have our designer labels *and fashion skills.*

If all else fails, at least we will always have our designer labels *and fashion skills.*

If all else fails, at least we will always have our designer labels *and fashion skills.*

If all else fails, at least we will always have our designer labels and fashion skills.

If all else fails, at least we will always have our designer labels *and fashion skills.*

If all else fails, at least we will always have our designer labels and fashion skills.

If all else fails, at least we will always have our designer labels *and fashion skills.*

If all else fails, at least we will always have our designer labels *and fashion skills.*

If all else fails, at least we will always have our designer labels *and fashion skills.*

If all else fails, at least we will always have our designer labels *and fashion skills.*

If all else fails, at least we will always have our designer labels *and fashion skills.*

If all else fails, at least we will always have our designer labels *and fashion skills.*

If all else fails, at least we will always have our designer labels *and fashion skills.*

If all else fails, at least we will always have our designer labels *and fashion skills.*

If all else fails, at least we will always have our designer labels *and fashion skills.*

If all else fails, at least we will always have our designer labels *and fashion skills.*

If all else fails, at least we will always have our designer labels *and fashion skills.*

If all else fails, at least we will always have our designer labels *and fashion skills.*

If all else fails, at least we will always have our designer labels *and fashion skills.*

If all else fails, at least we will always have our designer labels *and fashion skills.*

If all else fails, at least we will always have our designer labels *and fashion skills.*

If all else fails, at least we will always have our designer labels *and fashion skills.*

If all else fails, at least we will always have our designer labels *and fashion skills.*

If all else fails, at least we will always have our designer labels and fashion skills.

If all else fails, at least we will always have our designer labels and fashion skills.

If all else fails, at least we will always have our designer labels *and fashion skills.*

.

If all else fails, at least we will always have our designer labels and fashion skills.

If all else fails, at least we will always have our designer labels *and fashion skills.*

If all else fails, at least we will always have our designer labels *and fashion skills.*

If all else fails, at least we will always have our designer labels *and fashion skills.*

If all else fails, at least we will always have our designer labels *and fashion skills.*

If all else fails, at least we will always have our designer labels *and fashion skills.*

If all else fails, at least we will always have our designer labels *and fashion skills.*

Note to self...
purchase a new journal